Open *Your* Eyes

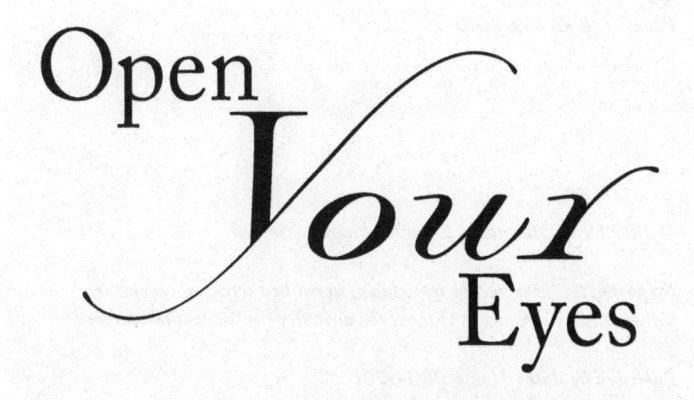

DR. G. ALEXANDER BRYANT

authorHOUSE

AuthorHouse™
1663 Liberty Drive
Bloomington, IN 47403
www.authorhouse.com
Phone: 1 (800) 839-8640

© *2017 Dr. G. Alexander Bryant. All rights reserved.*

No part of this book may be reproduced, stored in a retrieval system, or transmitted by any means without the written permission of the author.

Published by AuthorHouse 06/14/2017

ISBN: 978-1-5246-9560-6 (sc)
ISBN: 978-1-5246-9567-5 (e)

Print information available on the last page.

Any people depicted in stock imagery provided by Thinkstock are models, and such images are being used for illustrative purposes only. Certain stock imagery © Thinkstock.

This book is printed on acid-free paper.

Because of the dynamic nature of the Internet, any web addresses or links contained in this book may have changed since publication and may no longer be valid. The views expressed in this work are solely those of the author and do not necessarily reflect the views of the publisher, and the publisher hereby disclaims any responsibility for them.

Scripture quotations marked KJV are from the Holy Bible, King James Version (Authorized Version). First published in 1611. Quoted from the KJV Classic Reference Bible, Copyright © 1983 by The Zondervan Corporation.

DEDICATION

All glory, honor and praise to my Lord and Savior Jesus Christ who birthed in my spirit the messages written in this book. It is he who has made me who I am and without him I could not do anything.

To my wife, Yvonne De, thank you for compiling these messages. I appreciate you standing by my side supporting the vision God has given me. Love you.

To my mother, Mildred Bryant, who has encouraged me and shown immeasurable support throughout my life and ministry. Your sacrifices have not gone unnoticed.

Love to my sisters Carlotta Anthony and Dorothy Trimble, may you be blessed and strengthened.

I especially dedicate this book in memory of my sister, Paulette Bryant, who was a pillar in my ministry. The Lord took her in March 1984 but she will never be forgotten.

Dr. G. Alexander Bryant

My children Gregory, Jr., Titus, Sheranda, Shawana, Tiffany, Antwoine and all my beautiful grandchildren, I love you.

A heartfelt thank you to my Apostolic Sons and Daughters at A Place of Destiny Fellowship International in Atlanta and all the churches I oversee in The More Than Conquerors Fellowship International, Inc. for your support, love and prayers.

To my friends, associates and fellow laborers in the gospel, I pray you are blessed and encouraged as you peruse the pages of this book and apply the principles. May you be endowed with life changing experiences.

CONTENTS

Introduction ix

Chapter 1   "Get A Vision"..1

Chapter 2   "Stay Focused"...3

Chapter 3   "A Strong Mind vs. A Weak Mind"..........5

Chapter 4   "The Paradigm Shift".................................9

Chapter 5   "It's Time To Shift Because You Have Treasure In You"..11

Chapter 6   "Benefits"...13

Chapter 7   "Open Your Eyes" Part I 15

Chapter 8   "Open Your Eyes" Part II........................17

Chapter 9   "Open Your Eyes" Part III 21

Chapter 10 "I'm Not Barren Anymore" 25

Chapter 11 "You Will Get Through This" 29

Chapter 12 "God Is Going To Do The Impossible For You" 33

Chapter 13 "The Lord Will Be With You" 37

Chapter 14 "There Is More Power From On High" ... 41

Chapter 15 "Suddenly!" 45

INTRODUCTION

God wants you to excel in life. Be yourself and stop seeing and talking about what is wrong. Talk about what is right, *Righteousness exalts a nation*…Do not dialogue in negativism. We were designed to talk about "God the Good." Stop talking about the problem if you are not going to solve it. We have a Kingdom agenda not a religious agenda.

My assignment is to develop the total Christian man and Christian nature through scripture. I am here to help build your love walk and faith walk to think, believe, and trust God for anything realizing no one and no thing has power over you. I challenge you to Open Your Eyes to make sure you understand what God has provided for you. God will not allow you to remain in a dry situation. Do not be led by sight but be committed, dedicated and loyal. Become obedient and consistent for God will always produce. Fasting and prayer still works. God's desire is we live a heathy, happy and prosperous life. Change your mind from being so human and move to a mindset of more spiritual. Walk in unconditional love. Remember you have been made in the image of God and after His likeness; therefore, you do not need to have so many human experiences but have more spiritual experiences.

You are an heir to the promises of God. Don't worry. You have not been praying and waiting in vain. Be assured God will hear and answer (Micah 7:5-7). He will not let you down. Do not look to people. Look to Jesus and Him alone. Be careful who you are in covenant with. God is our source and forget not his benefits. Expect more. God is going to pay you. Keep going – stay and get everything due you. Leave the thoughts of the past and do not allow people to keep reminding you of past mistakes. God will satisfy your mouth with good things and good experiences. You must close down negative words. Dismiss them and do not repeat them. No one can curse what God has blessed. Declare that you will live and be happy!

This book is a compilation of only a few of the messages God has given me. I pray as you read each chapter you will become empowered, motivated and strengthened to Open Your Eyes and Live in Your Now.

CHAPTER 1

"Get A Vision"

James 1:2 declares to count it all joy when you fall into various temptations. God is trying to promote, build character and integrity that he can move for you and shift your spirit. Give God praise because you did not lose your mind. Your mind is a terrible thing to lose. Count it all joy. Wait on the Lord and rest in him. He will back up His Word. Tell God and thank him for your mind. Refuse to allow anyone to intimidate you. Be strong in the faith. Do not allow yourself to be stuck. Want something more than cash, clothes, and cars. Stop letting money be an issue. God rules supreme in your life. Think and allow him to speak through you. Go beyond the road blocks. It is more to God than what you see, hear, read, and know. Stop allowing your age to stop, block and hinder you. Tell yourself, I will not die like this…I refuse to die like this… God is better than this.

Do not settle being defeated by the enemy. You have gone through much, suffered too much, cried too much. Get everything God has spoken. Be strong in the Lord; be fearless…greater is he in you than he that is in the world… fight the good fight of faith. Look up, straighten up, and pick yourself up.

Get a Vision! Miracles will return to the House of God through no name people because the power of God is still the same. Speak to the cancer, diabetes, high blood pressure, heart condition to be gone. God is on the move… *For it is written, eye have not seen, nor ear heard, neither have entered into the heart of man, the things God hath prepared for them that love him. I Corinthians 2:9.*

You are unstoppable, no thing or no one can stop you. Whatever you are believing God for is coming. Success is in your future; God is for you. I admonish you to walk in optimism for God has all the answers.

CHAPTER 2

"Stay Focused"

Do not stay stuck in the moment. Words are voice activated. Agree with the Word of God. The Word will bring a change to the inner man. Believe your life is going to get better. Believe the Law of God above your current situation. This is your year of victory. Believe you are coming out with the victory. You are a winner, you are an overcomer, you cannot be defeated. Look to Jesus, the author and finisher of your faith. He is a restorer, a deliverer, your Savior.

There is a shifting of government (order). Focus on God the Good. God is going to bring you out so do not worry how you will get there. If you want a change, you have to talk. Your heart has to change. God always makes a way. Think Victory…that the situation, the challenge is no longer ruling you but you are ruling it. Your faith will get you out anything. If God allowed you to get in it He can get you out of it. God has given you the authority to speak His Word. Stop limiting yourself. Your mind is strong and powerful. There are endless possibilities. Believe God and step out on faith.

Change with information. Christ is never defeated. Do not die until your assignment is finished. You do not have to die until you want to, until the assignment is done, therefore, stop fearing dying. Command that negative situation to leave and be removed. Prophesy to the dead thing. Always remember, *THE WORD WILL WORK IF YOU WORK IT!*

Luke 18:27 declares that we should not deal with a spiritual thing with flesh. Talk to the spirit and curse the root of it leaving the flesh alone. *We wrestle not against flesh and blood but against principalities, powers, against the rulers of darkness of this world, against spiritual wickedness in high places (Ephesians 6:12).* War with the Word of God in the name of Jesus. God wants us free, happy and healed. Ignore distractions. Prophetic Winds are blowing in your life: good health, long life and favor. Be demanding, decreeing, declaring and believing something good is coming out of this. This is your Year of Victory. Spirits that come abnormal, not God given, come to paralyze your destiny. Keep fighting the good fight of faith. You will overcome. When you cannot handle the problem, take it to Jesus. Operate in the power God has released to you and Stay Focused!

CHAPTER 3

"A Strong Mind vs. A Weak Mind"

(Ephesians 6:10; II Timothy 3:1; Jude 1:4; Philippians 4:8)

Your mind has to be strong. A strong mind will produce insight, ability, endurance, perseverance, and war off evil forces. Strong in the Greek means to have the ability to stand against the odds. Think for yourself. Make Kingdom decisions. Guard your ear gates. Take authority (power) over evil spirits. Evil men and evil women open themselves up to evil spirits. They are not God conscious but impostures with hidden agendas. The Spirit of God carries character. Be a thinker; watch, observe, be strong minded and do not allow people to trick you. Walk in wisdom, determination, insight, empowerment, and strength.

We must believe our confessions. Our confessions should be based on the Word of God. The Word should change our thoughts and be in our mind as well as in our mouth. We should be growing, be wise and not tricked or deceived. Be honest and walk in integrity. Do not allow people to guide you denying the sovereign God (Jude 4). Have a forgiving heart. God wants our mind strong giving over only to the plan of God.

Do not have a weak mind. Be careful what you talk about and think. Train your mind to think good thoughts. Do not gossip, listen to gossip, or allow gossip to infiltrate your spirit but obey the scriptures. Consider why the person speaking to you is giving you that information. Why are they volunteering that information? Is the information being disseminated praise worthy? Then do not allow people to put things in your heart against the Word of God. No one has control over you but God. If what you hear is not to edify or build up, disassociate yourself and keep the right motives.

Bring your mind and spirit under the authority of God. Keep declaring and decreeing the scriptures…change your thoughts and apply the scriptures. Sometimes it takes getting from under stress, drinking plenty of water, getting up in the morning with an agenda, taking vitamins, getting plenty of sleep and changing your diet (Philippians 3:16).

You will have a strong mind and be unstoppable (impossible to stop or prevent from accomplishing a task, unbeatable, cannot be conquered) if you walk in faith and apply the principles I am giving. Whatever comes up realize God has it. You will be so anointed you cannot even stop yourself. See victory and not defeat. Believe God. He has already given us a way of escape. Whatever the situation, you will not die in it. Always stay in thanksgiving. God wants us to fight the good fight of faith because we are coming out regardless of the season. Guard your heart and your anointing. Try not to react in flesh. Ignore Satan. You are more than a conqueror. Step out on the Word. God will fight for you. Be available and be equipped.

God spoke to me and said, "nothing shall remain the same, I am doing a new thing." That includes you. God is on your side. He wants to take you from good to great; great to greater and greater to greatest. God is pulling you from the dark places to the place of peace where he is (Ezekiel 37:24). Refuse to go backwards. He is bringing us back from the dead, so enter into thinking of your now! You are not limitless or restricted. You shall have whatsoever you say. Do not be intimidated with the time and success of others. God has a fixed, set, appointed time to deal with each of us. Look to be successful in every area of your life. Whatever you touch should prosper.

CHAPTER 4

"THE PARADIGM SHIFT"

God wants us to move. Be prepared for what He is saying now and change the way you are thinking. Paradigm refers to change the way you are thinking, your habits, ideas, behavior, your mind (*Luke 8:22-25; Mark 4:35*). Change from familiar to unfamiliar. An epiphany means to become alert instantly seeing things clearer. Become a student of change. Launch forth…do not stay where you are. God is calling for a paradigm shift.

Do not perceive God like you once did. Live in peace. Trust God enough to shift. He knows what is best for you (*Matthew 8:23-27*). Storms come to confuse you. Even when God speaks, follow the instructions. You will still be challenged but follow the Word of the Lord (*Luke 8:23*). When you go through storms, it purifies you because God is in the storm with you. Do not quit regardless. He releases strength. We are shaped by our paradigms. You are surrounded by thoughts in your subconscience. Habits are formed from the thoughts in your sub-conscience and as a result will be your outcome. Do not be afraid of the paradigm shift. Read and study the Word then prepare.

Learn – Unlearn – Relearn. Why are you fearful? God will bring you to it then He will bring you through it. Know that God is always with you. He will never leave you nor forsake you. He is there always even until the end. No weapon formed against you will prosper, shake it off and go forward. Know who you are and what God has invested in you. God wants you better.

It's just a matter time. You must grow into the knowledge of new things. God deals with us individually. Embrace your uniqueness as long as you are not in error.

CHAPTER 5

"It's Time To Shift Because You Have Treasure In You"

Joshua 1:9; II Timothy 1:7; Proverbs 23:7; Psalm 27:3

Shift your thinking. Treasure is coming after this season... that accumulation of hidden wealth. Prepare your mind and not focus on the negative. Stay on your assignment to get to your destination. There is treasure in you: peace, health, stress free life, joy, sound mind, clear directions, knowing who you are, healing, valuable anointing. There is more to you than what you see. The enemy is after your mind. Our minds are being oppressed by things we do not understand. LIVE! Live through it. God gave us power... it's only a test.

Command fear to leave you. Resist and dismiss fear. Think free, victorious; realize you are valuable to God. *Trust in the Lord and lean not to your own understanding.* Don't get old when God is in control. Get up in the morning and speak Life over yourself. You should live as long as you want to live. Step out on faith. If you fail, get up and try again. Use what God has given you. Always remember, God loves you.

Stay focused on the positive…be connected with the things of the Kingdom. Maintain your fellowship with God. Don't be a busy body, talkative about things that do not concern you. Listen to the voice of God and be happy. God does not want us in constant warfare. He created us perfect and whole. God is in control…the government shall be upon His shoulder. Focus on the assignment God gives you. Give time over to prayer and supplication with thanksgiving. Rest in God, He has a set time to manifest what he promised.

Do not participate in evil. Speak well of people, do good, desire peace and go after it that you may prosper. Do what is right. Talk to God more, read your Bible and forgive more. There is treasure in you, so be careful what you think. What you think can produce a favorable or unfavorable outcome and affect your life style.

CHAPTER 6

"Benefits"

God wants us to experience and have a life of happiness, good health, wealth, prosperity, success, wisdom, and the anointing. This is for those that are submitted and committed to his Lordship. *(Psalm 103:1-5; Matthew 5; Psalm 104:1; Psalm 130:8; Psalm 107)*

There are benefits for walking with God when we give up worldly pleasures. Do not forget his benefits. There are pleasures in the world but they will not last. Talk good about Jesus. Leave the millenniums with a testimony that God is a healer, prosperous and successful God.

Your money is put on an assignment, a mission when you sow in the Kingdom…circulate it. It comes back to you 100 fold if you give with the right motive. It is a promise that God heals all our diseases, forgives all our sins and problems. They will no longer rule. God's Word will not return unto him void. Whatever appears in your life now and in the future, God will redeem you from it.

Favor surrounds us as a shield…it is a benefit. Jesus came to satisfy us and renew us like the eagle who is strong, flies constantly and soars above the storms of life.

God has some great things for us. Wait on him and believe. Hold on to what God said. Train in righteousness. Tell people the truth in righteousness and leave the decisions up to them. Never forget God's benefits and what is available for you. Bond with God's Word and let his Word think through you (*Isaiah 40:8*).

CHAPTER 7

"OPEN YOUR EYES"

Part I

We struggle because of lack of knowledge. Choices bring consequences. Think before making your choices. We will never understand all the things of God. He is a mystery. Think – Listen - Get Understanding. Consult the Lord and remember He loves us so much. Acknowledge the Lord in all your ways (before the decision is made) and Wait. He will direct your path. God has you! Let Him handle it.

God has not abandoned you. Live! According to *Exodus 17:15*, He is Jehovahnissi: God our banner, defender, protector, battle ax, victory. Open Your Eyes and see the beauty, awesomeness, and greatness of God. Yes, you are coming out with the victory…you cannot be defeated. See yourself in a victorious, wealthy, and healthy place. Put God first. God has a plan. God does not want life to be difficult. In *Genesis 16:13-14*, God sees (knows) YOU. He remembers and will not forget. God hears and sees. He will take care of you. The Lord looks out for you. Your best days are before you.

There are better days after this…open your eyes. Life is worth living because Jesus lives. You can make it. You cannot die. God gives us life. *I shall not die but live… (Psalm 118:17)*. Be happy, blessed, healed, whole, successful, wise, holy and prosperous. Don't die early, die when you get ready…Open Your Eyes and you will find what you lost.

Isaac means laughter…God is going to make you laugh. Get ready to laugh. Look beyond the dust and dirt and see the beauty coming. Don't get stuck with the current. See yourself better. Have a plan for your life. Declare that you are not stuck…you are developing and have so much better coming to you. Be a go getter. Reinvent yourself and see yourself further than where you are. I cannot emphasize it enough that no one is better than you. What you are dealing with is caught in the thickness of the trial, the pain and circumstances. Look into the thickness. So much living is inside you. See what God is saying. Get your spiritual equilibrium on track. There is a person in you that has not been discovered yet. God has not brought you this far to leave you. Don't forget God loves you. Open your eyes and keep on living.

CHAPTER 8

"OPEN YOUR EYES"

Part II

Get your own identity. Your Earthly Father and Apostolic Father give you your identity. Do not live your life through another individual. You are fighting from within if you are really gifted. Demons are attacking on the right and on the left. Forces are coming from your romance, health, finances and so many other areas but you have to make up your mind to live for God. Open Your Eyes…this is not your final destination. It is more to you than what you are currently experiencing. *Luke 24:45* lets us know we do not have to be satisfied where we are but want more… more God, more harmony, more unity, understanding, love, spiritual maturity. God is greater than anything that we are experiencing now. Be aware of what God is saying in this season. Don't be stuck…Open Your Eyes and see God.

If you do not open your eyes you will live beneath your privileges, be worn out with the cares of this world, discouragement will set in, you will become aggravated with people not being motivated, confused by your surroundings, complaining, have nothing good to say about anyone, have mood swings and ultimately die prematurely. It's all about God. *If thou faint in the day of adversity, thou strength is small (Proverbs 24:10).* God will open your understanding to the scripture, life and yourself. God did not design us to be miserable. God did not save you to make you unhappy. No one can run you out the House of God when you have an Apostolic seed inside. When you are after the heart of God, God will never let the enemy overcome you. When Jesus opens your understanding, you are no longer in the dark. Take a stand for righteousness. Want everything God has for you. Let your struggle be a private struggle. You are valuable. You should never be more happier in the world than in the Kingdom.

Nothing can stop you. *(Ephesians 1:18)* Don't be saved and unhappy. Don't play with your soul. Ignore foolish things. Be honest and tell the truth. Know the times an seasons and live a better life. Know the "hope" concerning you. You must see some hope before seeing your failures. It is not over. God has something better for you. Open Your Eyes and look for something better. Wake up in the morning and see better. Find consolation in God's Word. God will be with us even until the end of the world *(Matthew 28:20).*

If you Open Your Eyes, you will see something bigger, better, greater, powerful, awesome, wonderful. Look until fear, stress, and disappointment leave you. God is bigger, greater, and stronger. Better days are here. Do not accept what you see *(Mark 8:24)*. Keep looking and don't stop looking… Sooner or later something is going to break, something is going to turn in your favor. Do not limit yourself. Open Your Eyes and see what God is about to do. See the beauty of God, the plans He has for you. Have a vision for your own life. Follow God wholly like Joshua. When you Open Your Eyes, you see things like they ought to be and you will know how to live and be in peace. Embrace your uniqueness.

Five Scriptures that will revolutionize your life:

Matthew 10:35
Romans 8:28, 29
Galations 2:20
Philippians 4:11-13
James 1:2-4

CHAPTER 9

"OPEN YOUR EYES"

Part III

Open Your Eyes and look in the right places. You will see a new, free, happier, stronger, and blessed you. Your eyes are closed even when they are open if you are thinking negatively. Your eyes are windows to the soul. Change your status, mindset and what you are getting. What you send out is what you receive. Look at your perception. Some things are hidden from you because of where your mind is especially when your mind is already made up. Walk by faith and connect with the Word of God, what God says. Do not repeat the same things. God is our spiritual father and he does not want you the same. It is more to you than what you are producing. God has something better. See it before you get it (visualization – see it, dream it, receive it). Open your eyes. God will make your situation a haven of peace and a haven of rest. When you Open Your Eyes you shake off stress, fear, worry, and negative elements. God wants us to know what He has for us. God wants us to travel in peace. When you carry peace you carry peace everywhere you go. The atmosphere changes because of the peace you are carrying.

There is something unique about you. There is something in you that you can do that others cannot do. Others may become angry because God gave you that vision, blessing, gift, talent and not them. Tell them to see Jesus because you had nothing to do with it. Be assured that you are favored of God and to God be the glory. Open Your Eyes, good and great things are out there. If you open your eyes you will live, be powerful, successful, great, and you will not struggle. Refuse to live like this and allow Satan to snatch everything from you. Do not just wish and hope but know and experience. God wants us to know there is more than what you are experiencing. Do not limit yourself. *Greater is he that is in you than he that is in the world.* Do not just quote the Word and stay the same but open your eyes and walk in inspiration, excitement, faith and strength out of Zion.

We are riding on the strength of God because our physical bodies could not handle the things we have encountered. God is going to show up and show out in the midst of your challenges. He is our defender. He is sending the rod of his strength to vindicate us. Open your eyes and see who God really is. You know God in the furnace of affliction when you open your eyes. Do whatever God gives with joy and in the timing he has requested. When your eyes are not open you operate in what you think, feel and begin to pattern after people rather than after the Word, limiting yourself.

People have their own concepts how Christendom is and who God is. It hinders miracles, signs and wonders. Have a heart for God not religion. God cannot move with different mindsets. Listen and obey what God says... Open Your Eyes.

See the splendor of God. God wants us to experience what he has for us. He has equipped us with what we needed when we were born again. It is already there but it is being discovered. It is not in heaven, it is in you. If you do not open your eyes, you will be defeated. When your eyes become opened you know you do not wrestle against flesh and blood. You see what no one else sees. Dare to believe and trust God in the face of adversity. Know how powerful you are in God. Rise to the occasion. God will set you up for victory and success. Do not have a "faggot spirit", whether you are male or female, sowing discord, justifying your wrong doings and pointing to someone else so people will not look at you.

Open your eyes, it is all about God. When you open your eyes, you operate in the spirit of humility, praying more. It is time to seek God like never before. Keep your spirit right and value what you are carrying. Open your eyes and come forth with power. See and change for the better.

CHAPTER 10

"I'M NOT BARREN ANYMORE"

I Samuel 1:18, 19 – Hannah cried, prayed and begged God for a child.

During my research, there were at least seven women in the Bible identified as barren (unable to have children). I would like to focus on four of these women: Sarah, Rebekah, Rachel and Hannah. It was a shame for a married woman during this period in time not to be able to bear a child for her husband. Hannah cried, prayed, and begged God for a child. She was a woman of prayer and went yearly to the house of the Lord. She was grateful and kept her vows to God. Hannah was very humble even though she was jealous of her husband's second wife, Pennineh, who was able to bear children.

Let's look at just these four women mentioned above. At the set time, God promised each of them a child. Yet barren, these women each reacted differently when God promised them a child. Sarah laughed, Rebekah questioned God in doubt and unbelief, Rachel put all the blame and responsibility on her husband, but Hannah prayed. She was exceptional and chose to trust God. She did not allow anything to abort her desires. She was different. Hannah was unblemished in character. God had a plan and purpose for her life. When He opened Hannah's womb, she not only gave birth to one child, Samuel, whose name in the Hebrew meant "heard by God" but she gave birth to three more sons and two daughters. She was not barren any more. God answered her prayers. This leads you to know you are never too old to receive. If God did it for these women and he is the same God yesterday, today and forever, why can't he do it for you? God is going to turn it around for you. He has not forgotten you.

Barren means unfruitful, sterile, unable to produce, deserted, without, empty of what's valuable to you, no results or achievements, useless. We are not barren anymore. God has impregnated us with vision. He has you…do not compare yourself to anyone. Hannah was barren but kept crying and praying until God answered her. So, keep crying out to God until you receive your answer.

God does not want you to live unhappy, defeated, stressful and in poverty. Change your thinking. In I Samuel 1:17-19, God is going to do what we request. In verse 18, Hannah received Dunamis (power) from talking to the Prophet, and in verse 19, she rose <u>early</u> in the morning and worshipped the Lord because she heard the Word from Eli. God is going to replace some things and put them where they need to be in your life. He is concerned about you.

Look to God to fulfill what is missing. He is concerned about the total man. God made you perfect and whole. Look to Jesus. God has not forgotten you…He will never leave you or forsake you. God has a plan for your life. Be desperate to get God's attention. Go to God, the one that can make a change, shift, deliver, make the situation better. Do it God's way to avoid unnecessary pain. God has so much more for you.

God is a protector, peace giver, life provider for us. Tell God that you are not wicked, you are His child. Ask Him not to let the curse of the wicked come upon you. Tell God he is the only one who can turn that difficult situation around *(Psalm 62:8)*. He will grant what we ask. Whatever you are barren of, God will replace it, redo, renew or create it. Receive this Prophetic Word, Act on it, Worship and God will answer. Conception is completed during the Worship.

Do not be intimidated by time, age or what other people have accumulated. Be assured of yourself and who you belong to. No one is better than you. If God wants you to have what others have He will provide it for you. Hannah heard the Word from Eli and connected with it. She rose early in the morning and worshipped and conception was made in the spirit realm. Then God remembered her and conception was made in the physical. Get in the presence of the Lord, stay there and watch how you will come out.

Dr. G. Alexander Bryant

Keep your mind on what you want God to do. Just believe. Desire manifestation and see it happening. Receive it and bless the Lord until manifestation comes because he has already given us access to the throne. Hold your peace. Be desperate. God will make it up to you. Hannah continued to cry out to the Lord until she received the promise from God of the petition she had before him. She was not barren anymore. I admonish you to continue believing and trusting God. Cry out to him and you will not be barren anymore.

Read these additional scriptures and I know you will be empowered with faith to believe God: Judges 18:6; Mark 5:34; Psalms 20:4, 5

CHAPTER 11

"You Will Get Through This"

Ezekiel 28:24; I Peter 4:14; Romans 5:3

You should be working on something to make your life better, to have more to shift your career. You should have a vision for your life and know God is not going to just leave you where you are when you love him.

Change where you are, what you think, what you once thought and what you believe. Go before God and work it out. Your relationship is between you and God and him only. God gave you your own DNA. Someone else may have your name but your DNA and Social Security number set you apart. No two individuals are exactly alike. Your salvation does not have anything to do with anyone but between you and God; therefore, mind your own business. Be free and do not compare yourself to no one else. You are different from anyone even in your family. God placed something unique in you. Embrace your uniqueness. Know what you are and who God is.

God will convince you he knows you and where you are. Make up in your mind to come to a conscious decision to walk with God. Keep going even if you have to go alone. Walk with God if tears come down, your best friend leaves, even if everything falls apart. Focus on what God says. Speak like Job, *"though he slay me, yet will I trust him" (Job 13:15)*. Wait until your change comes and know your season is going to shift. You will get through this regardless how dark your day looks and how cloudy your skies may become. It may not look like it and it may not seem like it but your season is changing. God sends a Word and activates it. His word will not return to him void. It has to work. The elements have to obey what God gives. You are going to get through this season.

Now, after you come out of this, you will walk in manifestation. Do not give up on yourself. Dream big and get a vision for yourself. You are getting through with favor, increase and abundance on you, not bitter or complaining. There may be things you cannot share and you may be wondering why God has not come through for you yet? God is saying, *"I am God and beside me there is no other."* You need a Word because demons are talking in your ears. I'm here to encourage you that the season of change is here. Go through it with joy, peace, understanding and victory. Nothing God allows you to go through is in vain. It is working together for your good. You are coming out this season of Baka (crying, weeping). According to II Corinthians 12:9, Jesus has gone before you and said his grace is sufficient for you and his strength is made perfect in weakness. You have what it takes to get through this season in your life because you accepted Jesus as your Lord and Savior. He graced you to get through with victory. Work the vision you have for your life. Let the old season go when the new season comes. Many times we focus on the weaknesses, the hardships and pain, rather than the God who can change it. Let it go for you will get through this.

Nothing just happens when you are a true believer. Look at the positive side. Stop putting yourself down. Every day is a celebration. Now get ready for divine intervention, spiritual motivation, fresh oil and the visitation of God in prophetic deptness. Get ready to live, be wealthy, focused, healthy and happy! Hear the heart of God and realize we do not die, we multiply.

CHAPTER 12

"God Is Going To Do The Impossible For You"

If you came this far, you need to see this through. Wait on God and do not fear. Let God do what He wants...you are going to be all right. Whatever you are experiencing will not take you out. You are not waiting in vain. God knows what it takes to build character. He knows what it takes to chisel off all the negative. The adversary says that God is not going to do what he said. Know that as long as God is with you, you can accomplish anything.

Be in tune with the voice of God (Joshua 23:14). Be faithful. Do not lean to your own understanding. Issues with your mind, health, and finances seem impossible but this is your stopping day. Give it to God and Rest in Him. God is sending Emergency Faith now! Resist the devil and ask God to lift your mind. God has a plan for your life and you should have a plan for your own life. God has chosen you. Be strong and focused enough to get what you need from him. Be conditioned to wait on God. Look into

Luke 1:30-35 and receive amazing information as well as a supernatural encounter.

It will come to pass…God will do the impossible! You are not laboring, waiting, suffering in vain. It is just a matter of time. This is our time to believe God. Your head must be clear. God is setting us up. Take the limits off yourself and stay open to God. This is your "Suddenly Season." This mission is possible. Say it to yourself until you believe it…God is doing the impossible for me right now!

The year of 2017 began with the impossible being possible: Donald Trump, a successful businessman, not a politician, becoming President of the United States of America (God allowed it), The Atlanta Falcons losing the Super Bowl, and the Academy Awards "Movie of the Year" being misquoted… God allowed it all.

God will cause to be what does not currently exist. This is the season God will cause to be our season of acceleration and not the season to doubt, walk in unbelief and be in conflict with anyone. Ignore craziness and walk away with victory!

Take a close look at Psalm 27. In the time of trouble, God will hide you that you do not look like what you have been through. Let the God part of you be real. Know who you believe and be persuaded he is able to keep that which is committed unto him (your mind).

God renews mercy every day. Goodness and Mercy shall follow you every day of your life. Be assured whose you are and who you are. Do not be robbed of what belongs to you.

God is not shocked by anything we do or anything that happens to us. Be real with God. Keep talking to him and eventually you will talk your way out regardless of how severe, embarrassing, and painful. God will keep us going. Your potentials are unlimited because of who you are. Once you are aware of this you can go anywhere. Did you know that you draw to you what you are aware of? Train your spirit to think and draw good things to you: happiness, money, joy, sound mind, healthy body and more.

The parables and teachings of Jesus have principles. Look for the principles in the parables. Learn the principles and you will never be defeated. Continue to focus on God the Good. He has advice, instructions and information. Psalm 27:7 shows us he led them out with power and in verse 9, he satisfied the longing souls with good things. Some things God will do for you so you will forget the bad that has happened. God has good things for us. He wants us to be happy, put a smile on our face, and remove the negative.

Keep crying out to God. Things have to change. Jesus is the living Word. "It", whatever you are experiencing, will not destroy you. Sooner or later he is going to do the impossible for you…it's just a matter of time.

CHAPTER 13

"THE LORD WILL BE WITH YOU"

II Chronicles 20:17

Do not worry about anything. God has already gone before you. He promised to be with you. We are being trained to war against spirits and not people for *we wrestle not against flesh and blood but against principalities, against powers, against the rulers of darkness of this world, against spiritual wickedness in high places (Ephesians 6:12)*. You may be an instrument or tool but you are not my enemy. It takes the anointing, God, power and discipline to be quiet. Silly people keep talking and have attitudes. You do not have to defend yourself. Let people come into the conclusion of what they want but be wise and discern spirits. Love tells you the truth and when you become mature it is between you, God and the other person. Be concerned about yourself. It is not your business to be nosey about someone else's affairs. Mind your own business. You should be working on something for your own success and well being.

Do not defend yourself with words. You do not have to fight in this battle because there is a changing of the guards. Listen to God. He is going to do the fighting for you. This year do not fight but focus on your health, money, affairs. Do not be so angry that you are unable to think clearly. Close your mouth sometimes…a quiet answer turns away wrath. Hold your peace. Fight only the good fight of faith. See God in every situation where the enemy has popped up. Do not worry about trying to get the last word in or defend yourself.

We do not wrestle against each other. The anointing and the assignment on your life is what the enemy is after. Do not give in but be strong. The enemy wants you to be aggravated and distracted that you will not hear the voice of God. God gives an Apostolic voice to identify who you are. We are not ordinary. God has hand-picked, chosen you. War in the spirit through faith. Do not let the enemy take over you. Demon spirits do not like righteousness. Demons operate "in order" when they devise their attack but the church is operating in division. Weakness helps demonic spirits go against the spirit of God. You cannot curse, argue and then pray. Do not get in the flesh. Demons must be cast out, not cursed and fussed out. Repent so God can hear you. Our mind and mouth should be clean. Do not get in the flesh and tie God's hands when you are attacked.

When you represent Jesus, opposing forces and attacks will come against you. Once you take a true stand, you will continue to be attacked. So, come in agreement and make a conscious decision to walk with God. Do not bring an open reproach to God and the church. You are carrying the Ark of the Covenant. The ark represents carrying the glory of God. Stop attacking your sister and brother. You cannot afford to be out of order. Have power in the glory. Keep your heart pure that you may keep Gods glory channeling through you. The enemy will do things you will not expect when he is targeting you.

You will not have to fight this battle…Set Yourself… position yourself in the Kingdom and prepare yourself in the spirit realm to attack. Allow God to fight for you. You have been anointed to go through what you have gone through, what you are going through and what you will go through.

STAND STILL - Do not be intimidated by anything or anyone. Know you have someone in your corner. God is fighting for you. Get out of the flesh and do it yourself with the help of the Lord your God. See the salvation of the Lord. FEAR NOT – just like it came it will leave. You do not have anything to fear. NOR, BE DISMAYED – Do not lose consciousness of who God is in a chaotic situation. God will take over if we do not get in the way… the Lord will be with you.

CHAPTER 14

"THERE IS MORE POWER FROM ON HIGH"

St. Luke 24:48, 49

The church is not in need of more tongues, another concert, more dancing or emotions but we need more power! Not more cameras, innovative things right now but souls are in need of more power from on high. The main ingredient the church is leaving behind is more power. Someone has a vision for beautiful edifices…that is wonderful but we are leaving behind what pleases God, Dunamis power!

You must have power to witness, draw and influence people in excitement and enthusiasm. Where are you going? Power doesn't come with paying tithes, coming to church, or traveling with the leader but power comes from spending time with God. When there is lack of power at work, people do not speak to you, they argue, get angry quick, have attitudes, debate and are not able to close their mouths and there is no unity. How much time are you spending on your face before God asking for power? When your soul is in need, you need more than clothes, cars, cash. You need power from on high.

During the time of this passage of scripture (Luke 24), there is a time of celebration, Feast of the Harvest, the Jewish Feast of Weeks. Jesus had established this celebration in the capital city for the people of God (50 days after the Passover/Easter – Pentecost). During this time Jesus walked on the earth and showed himself for 40 days according to Acts 1 and stepped on a cloud staying away 10 days. Wait on the Lord, call Jesus until he comes and changes your language, your nature, your mind. The Spirit of God, The Comforter, comes to comfort. So, why are you so easily disturbed, bothered, angered by contrary issues, things you do not agree with? He comes to calm, release, and restraint. He does not come to just make you feel good. If you cannot control your emotions, why are you disturbed even when you are right and the other person is wrong. The comforter comes to shake bad attitudes, cravings for weed, cursing, ungodly desires from the believer and fill your heart with Christ.

When you have power, the Lord keeps the house electrified with his glory. Allow God to fill you with his Spirit. (John 14:26, Acts 1:4, Acts 16:7) When you are filled with the Holy Ghost you have power. You have an urgency to get to the House of God where he is. In his presence you experience the fullness of joy. Power from on high causes you to do right, mind your own business, come to church, and tell the truth. The Comforter will be sent from the Father and is not contaminated by earth's germs but he is pure, whole, holy. He comes to take away sadness, sorrow, condemnation, anger, evil, filthy thinking and give deliverance, peace, healing, and taming that deadly poisoned tongue.

If you sit and listen to what the enemy is saying, he will tell you all kinds of things to do. You should have love, peace, wisdom, knowledge, kindness, longsuffering and stickability (Galations 5). It seems like the devil will anoint people to agitate you but resist him even if you have to change your environment. He wants you to carry out the thoughts he places in your mind especially when he knows you are fearless. I admonish you that when you are on your job walk like you are saved. No one will follow you when your testimony is tainted. The Holy Ghost comes to provide new information that you will learn through the information given and not repeat negative experiences. It will make you miserable and vexed repeating negative things over and over. Come to church that the Holy Spirit will bring confirmation, clarity, and understanding. Don't be repeat offenders. You must be taught because you are dealing with real live demons. When you come to the House, you will learn how not to allow flesh to override.

The truth will make you free and it does not judge. Come to the house so the spirit will bring the scripture back to remembrance. You will not lose your mind when someone jumps you. Do not get impatient or allow negative spirits to get in your ear. Do not analyze things in your intellect but get in the Holy Ghost. You are under the authority of God and you must live the life what you talk by the grace of God. God wants the people of God to wait for the promise. Allow Him to prove himself to you. Take time and wait on the Lord. Get desperate for God and do not leave until you get an answer. 120 waited in the Upper Room while 380 left before time. The Holy Spirit had not been released upon the earth yet. You must have the Holy Ghost. Water Baptism is important but it alone cannot save you.

Like water, it alone cannot clean you, you need soap. In Malachi 3:2, God was a fuller's soap, he washes everything out that should not be in you. Get on the altar until God purges you. If you are purged, you will not be lying, smoking dope, smoking cigarettes, dipping snuff and any other things against the laws of God. Your soul is more important. Do not worry about who is in the White House. Leave him alone if you are not going to pray for him. Focus on what you need…power from on high that will change you, cause an explosion to blow out all the old causing a new you to come forth walking in power, influence, success and victory.

CHAPTER 15

"SUDDENLY!"

The change will happen and happen SUDDENLY! I know you may be frustrated, disappointed, angry, tired but something is going to happen suddenly. I am talking to your spirit and not to your flesh or feelings. The breakthrough is coming suddenly, it is changing suddenly, rearranging suddenly, going to overturn suddenly, going to get better suddenly!

The Lord is saying it is not as long as it has been, it is coming suddenly. Acts 2:2-4 declares: *and suddenly there came a sound from heaven as of a rushing mighty wind, and it filled all the house where they were sitting. And there appeared unto them cloven tongues like as of fire, and it sat upon each of them. And they were filled with the Holy Ghost, and began to speak with other tongues, as the Spirit gave them utterance.* Have a hunger, thirst and craving in you knowing only God can fix it. Get tired of things as they are…going through the same motions and getting the same results.

Are you ready for a breakthrough? Jesus said, if you come to Him, He will in no wise cast you out.

Get desperate for a breakthrough, deliverance, change, help, strength, move of God, power. The Bible says, Suddenly, there was a sound. God is dealing with a sound: a holy sound, a heavenly sound, a sound like you have never heard before. You have heard many sounds but you have not heard this sound. God has a special sound that only prophetic people can hear. Come to the house and listen for a sound that will loose your shackles, set you free, close your bands, and heal your mind. First, there was "suddenly" and then there was "a sound" that came from heaven. Suddenly – a Sound – and it came from heaven! The sound you are listening for will not come from the city or from the college campus because it is coming from heaven.

That is why people cannot relate to our praise. Your praise is a heavenly praise…a praise that will shift your mind, set you up for a miracle, a breakthrough, change your life, change your walk, change your talk. It has to come from heaven as a quick, rushing wind coming with force.

It depends on how much hell and warfare you have been through, how much trouble you have had and how much the enemy has played with your mind. If you have been through much it has to come with a force that will knock everything out of you that the enemy has tried to set up inside you.

Sudden deliverance is coming with force: a powerful, mighty, strong, great wind that filled the whole house with cloven tongues of fire that sat on them. It is on its way to you – get ready…

Open Your Eyes

Your Deliverance is coming Suddenly,

and it's coming with WIND and FIRE!

Printed in the United States
By Bookmasters